FRYDERYK CHOPIN
IMPROMPTUS

FRYDERYK CHOPIN
COMPLETE WORKS

ACCORDING
TO THE AUTOGRAPHS AND ORIGINAL EDITIONS
WITH A CRITICAL COMMENTARY

EDITOR
IGNACY J. PADEREWSKI
ASSISTED BY
LUDWIK BRONARSKI
AND
JÓZEF TURCZYŃSKI

WITH REPRODUCTIONS OF
PORTRAITS
AND MANUSCRIPTS

MCMXLIX

THE FRYDERYK CHOPIN INSTITUTE
POLSKIE WYDAWNICTWO MUZYCZNE

FRYDERYK CHOPIN
COMPLETE WORKS

IV

IMPROMPTUS
FOR PIANO

EDITORIAL COMMITTEE
I. J. PADEREWSKI
L. BRONARSKI
J. TURCZYŃSKI

THIRTIETH EDITION

INSTYTUT FRYDERYKA CHOPINA
POLSKIE WYDAWNICTWO MUZYCZNE

MUSIC MATRICES PRODUCED
BY POLSKIE WYDAWNICTWO MUZYCZNE
TEXT SET IN PÓŁTAWSKI 'ANTIQUA' TYPE
PRINTED IN POLAND 2017
ISMN 979-0-2740-0013-4

JAKOB GOETZENBERGER - PENCIL DRAWING - 1838

AUTOGRAPH OF THE IMPROMPTU IN A FLAT MAJOR (BEGINNING)

AUTOGRAPH OF THE IMPROMPTU IN A FLAT MAJOR (BARS 16–30)

AUTOGRAPH OF THE IMPROMPTU IN A FLAT MAJOR (BARS 105–121)

IMPROMPTUS

Allegro assai, quasi Presto

Andantino

Vivace

Allegro agitato ($\bullet$ = 84)

IMPROMPTU

Allegro assai, quasi Presto

Op. 29

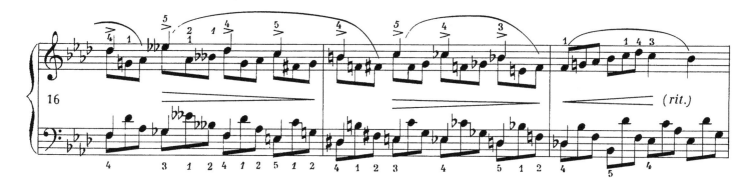

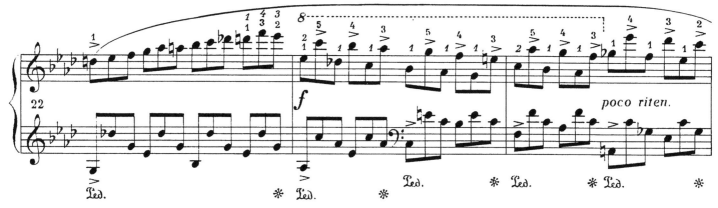

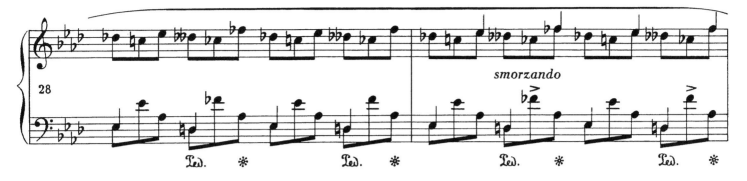

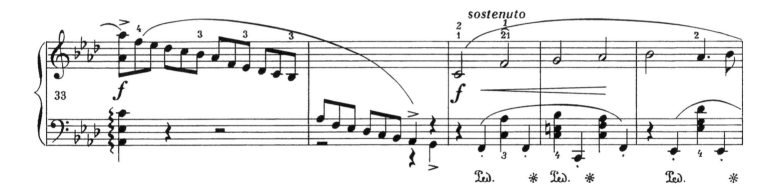

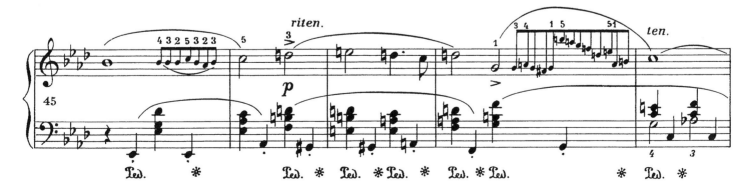

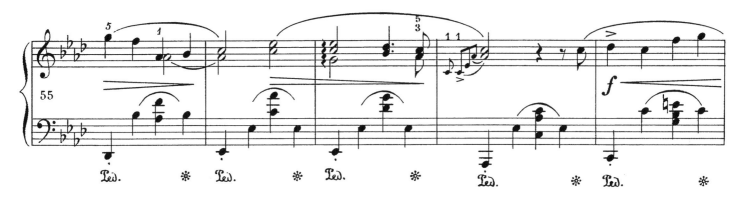

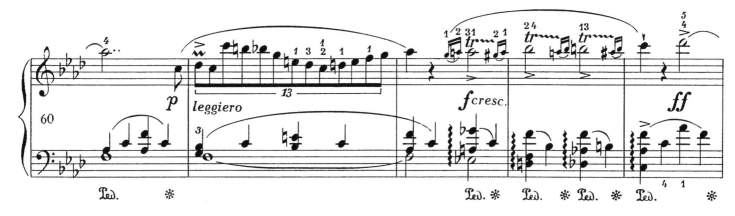

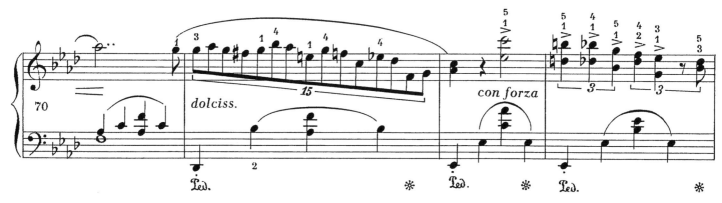

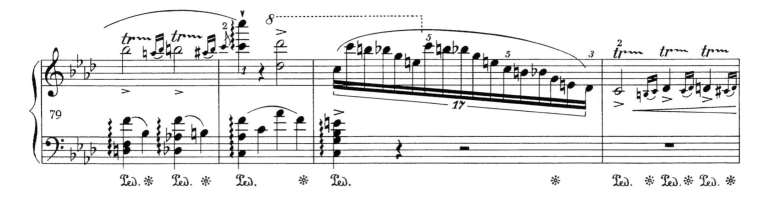

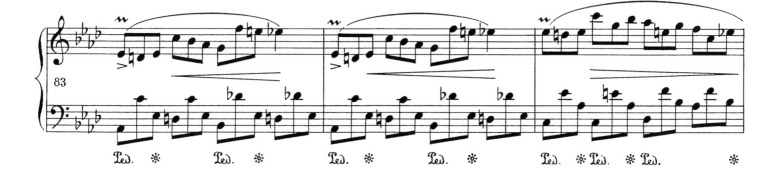

IMPROMPTU

Op. 36

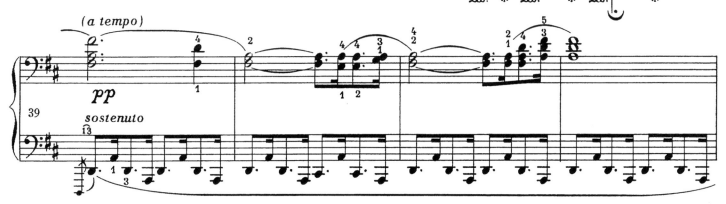

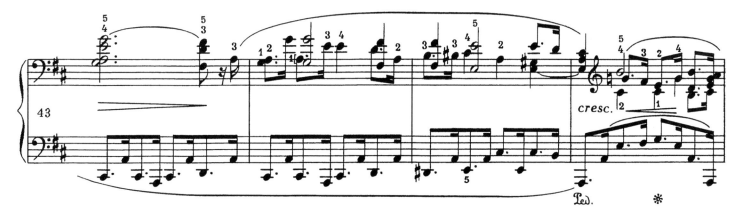

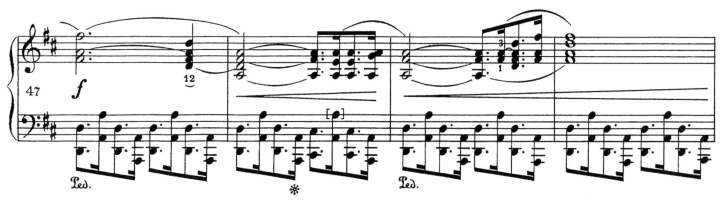

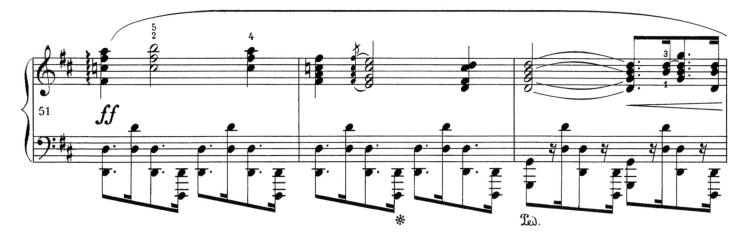

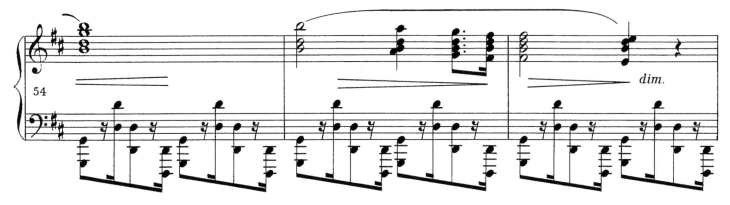

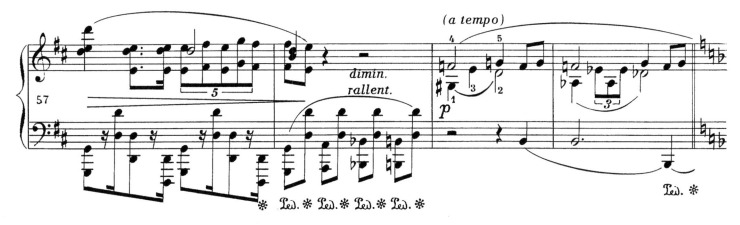

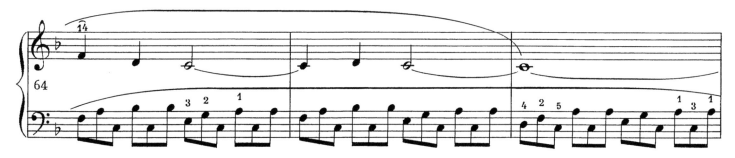

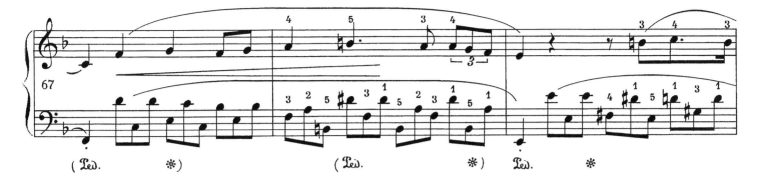

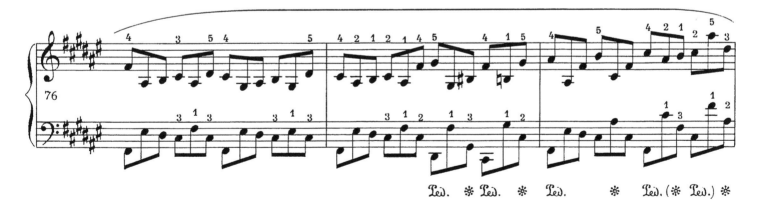

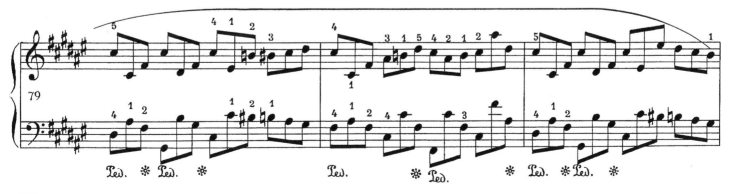

PWM - 233

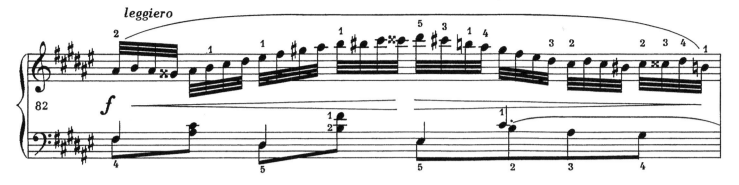

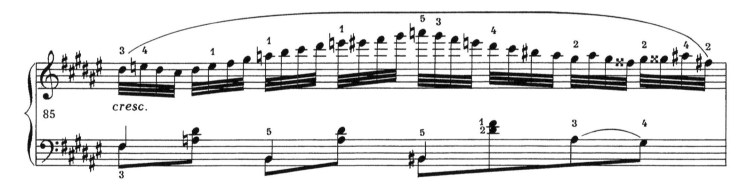

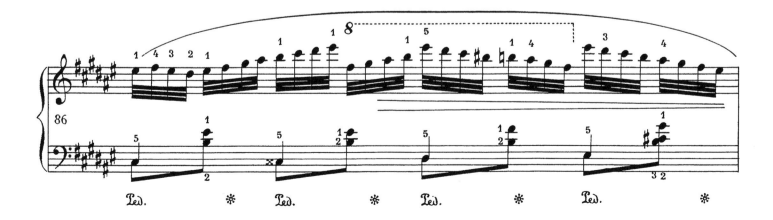

19

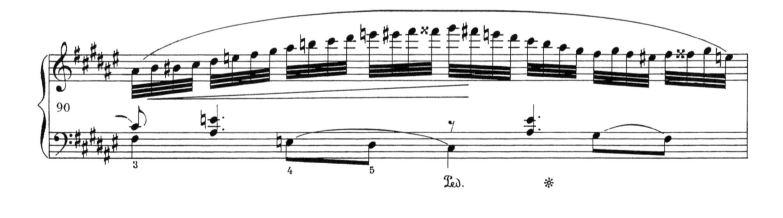

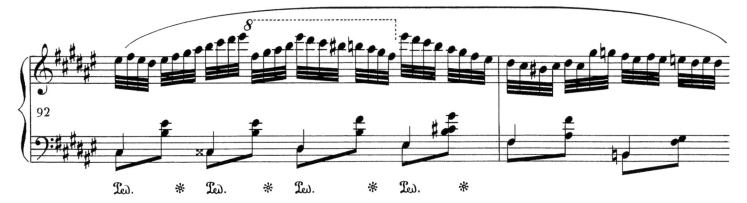

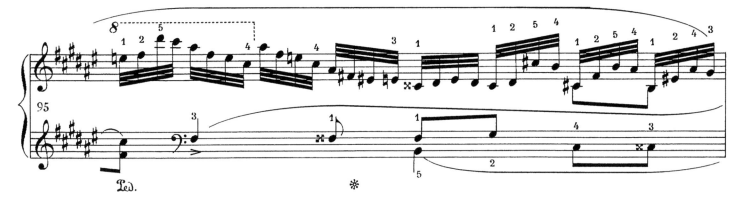

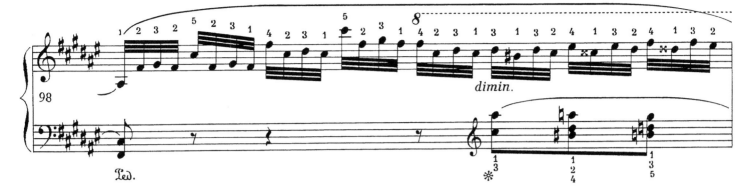

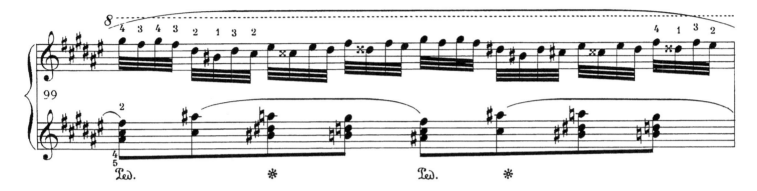

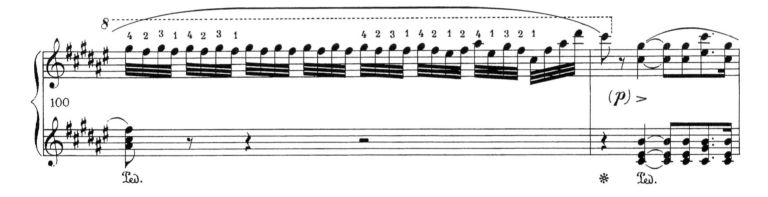

A Madame la Comtesse Esterházy, née Comtesse Batthyany

IMPROMPTU

Op. 51

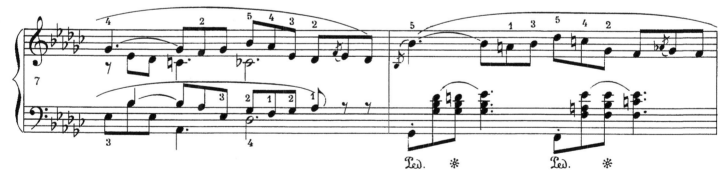

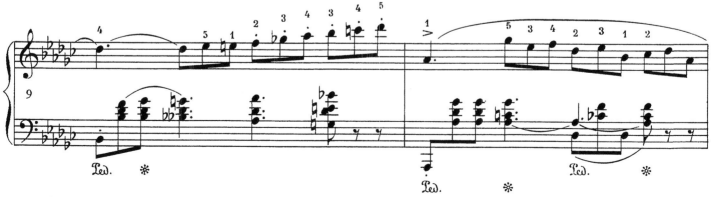

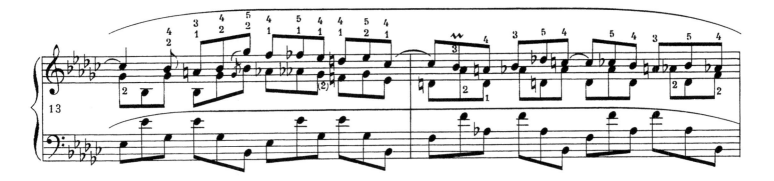

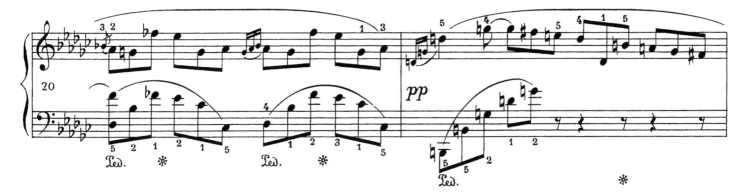

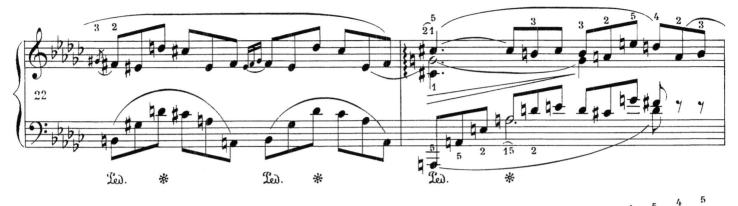

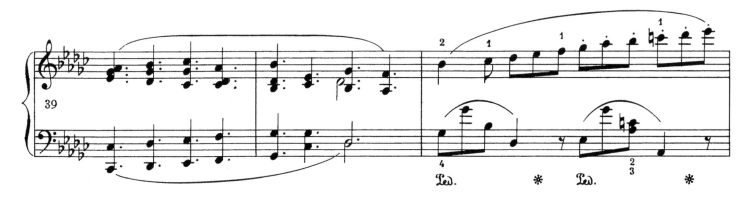

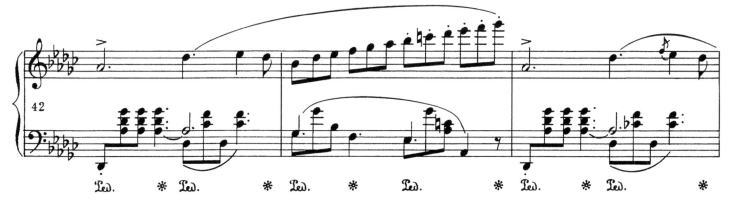

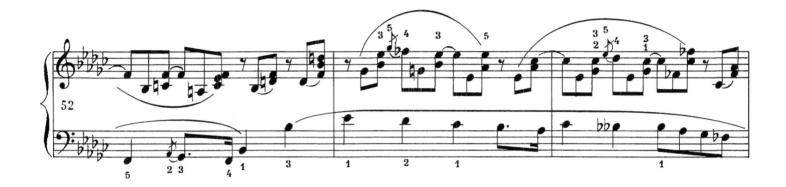

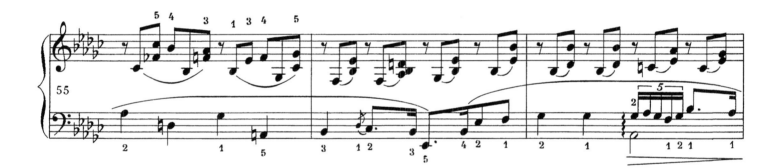

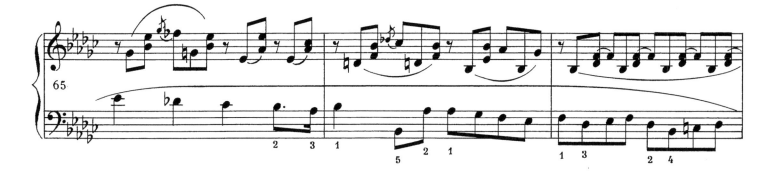

Tempo I

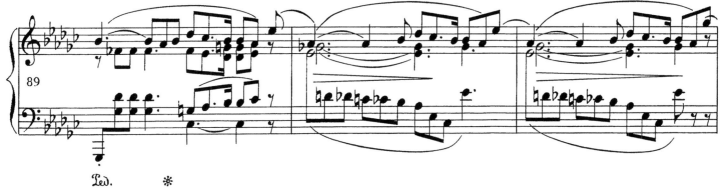

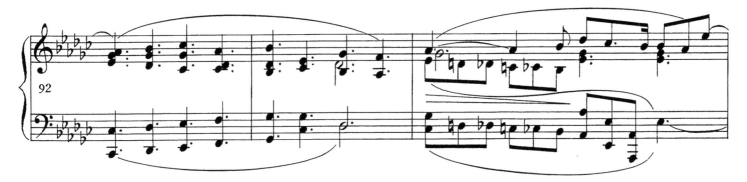

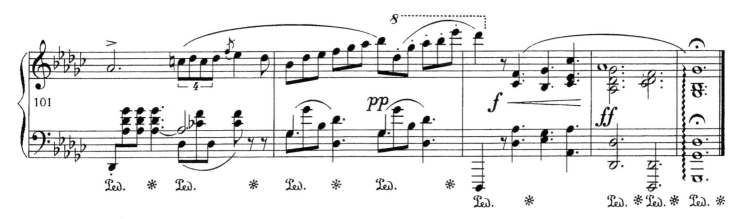

FANTAISIE-IMPROMPTU

Op. 66

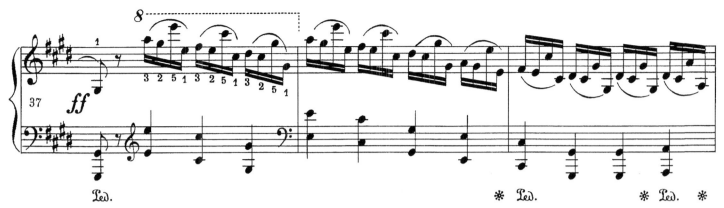

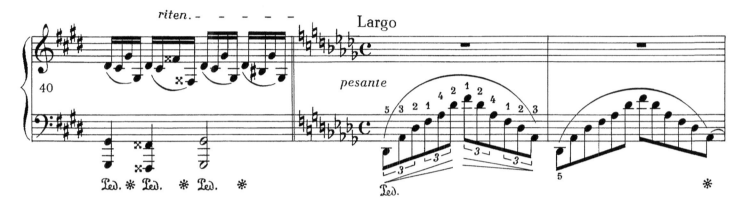

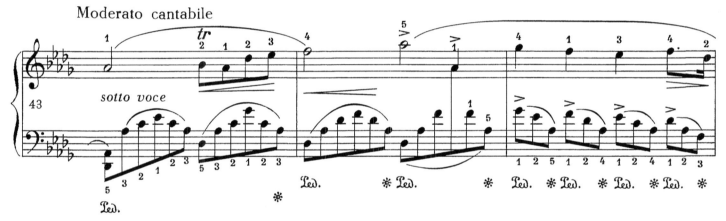

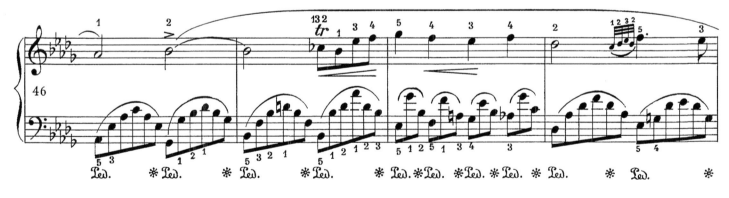

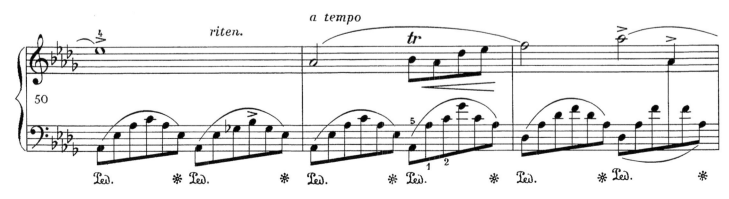

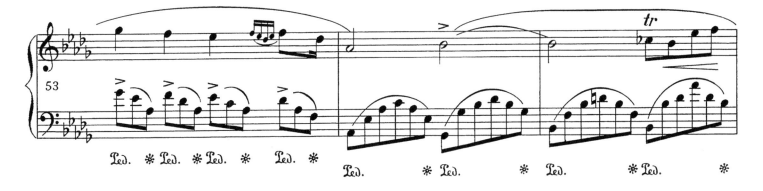

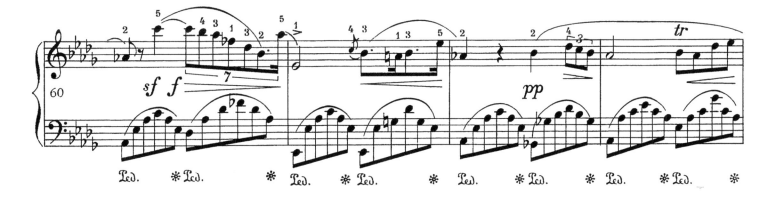

34

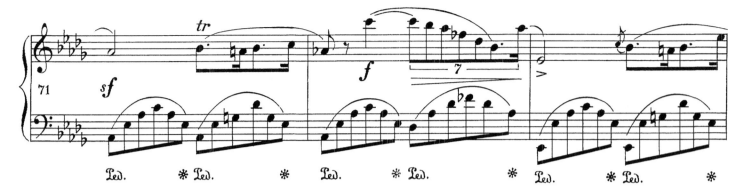

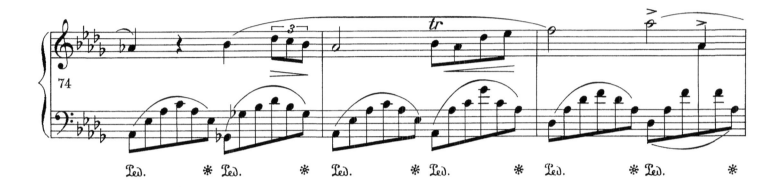

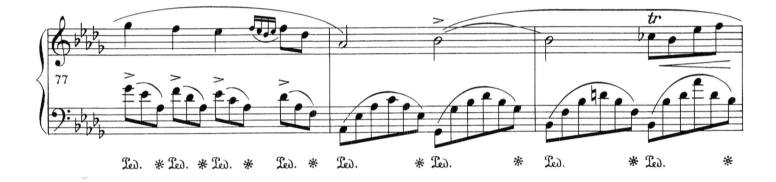

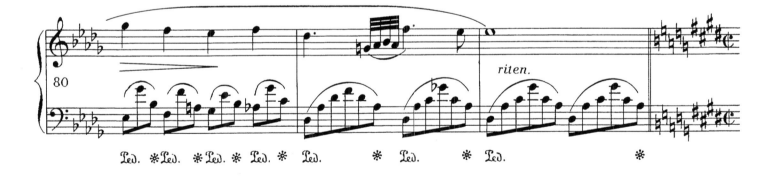

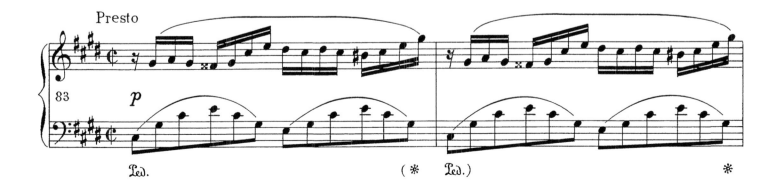

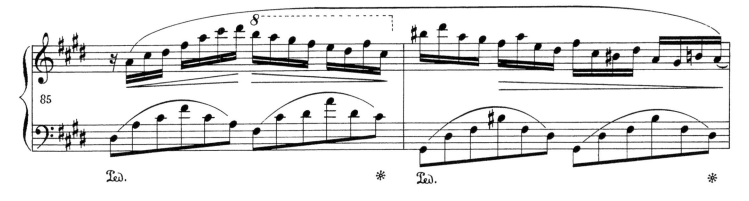

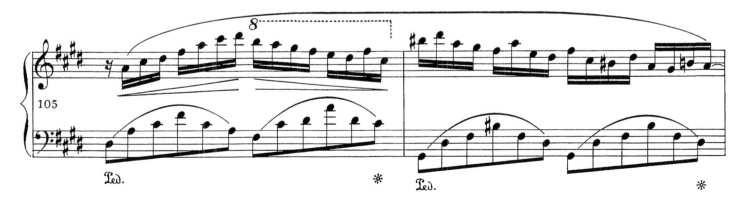

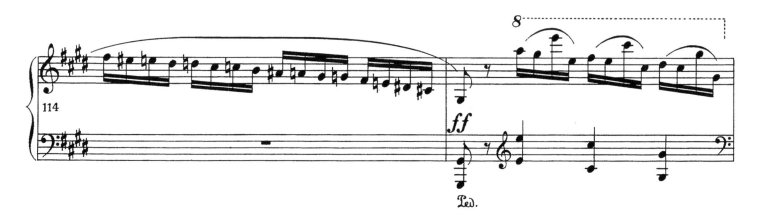

THE CHARACTER OF THE PRESENT EDITION

The principal aim of the Editorial Committee has been to establish a text which fully reveals Chopin's thought and corresponds to his intentions as closely as possible. For this reason the present edition has been based primarily on Chopin's autograph manuscripts, copies approved by him, and first editions. The Committee has had to take into account the fact that even though a manuscript may have served as a basis for a first edition, it is not always the final version of any particular piece. Chopin frequently changed details of his compositions up to the very last moment. So much is clear not only from contemporary sources, but also from variants between original editions and manuscripts. Such variants, moreover, cannot possibly be considered to be engraver's errors or editorial alterations. The manuscripts will always be the prime source for the textual verification of Chopin's works. But although no effort has been spared, it has not always been possible to discover or study a given manuscript. The Editorial Committee has also consulted recent editions for purposes of comparison.

When it has proved impossible to establish the authentic version or the one corresponding to Chopin's last intentions, any discrepancy has been carefully indicated in the Commentary.

Dynamic and agogic signs correspond to the manuscripts and first editions. Sometimes they have been supplemented by the repetition of signs appearing in identical or similar places. Other additions have been placed in brackets. Chopin's original fingering, rare though it is in the manuscripts and first editions, has been expressly indicated in the Commentary.

The pedal marks given by the Editorial Committee are strictly in accordance with the manuscripts and original editions. Certain insignificant modifications have been introduced, but only where this is required by the greater resonance of modern pianos, as well as in analogous passages or repetitions, where comparison has revealed inconsistency, or where correction or completion is required owing to mistakes or negligence. Chopin's pedal-marking is usually careful, precise, and in certain places very delicate, sometimes producing entirely new pianistic effects (e.g. at the beginning of the Polonaise-Fantasia). Those passages in which Chopin has not marked the pedalling are generally explained by the fact that the pedalling required is very simple, and is therefore self-evident; or, on the contrary, that it is so subtle as to be too complicated, if not impossible, to indicate In any case, the use of the pedal is a very delicate and entirely individual matter, depending on many factors, such as instrument, touch, tempo or acoustics of the room. For this reason, the Editorial Committee has decided to leave the pedalling as found in the original documents. This conforms with the principles adopted in the present edition.

In principle, Chopin's phrasing has been retained. But certain slurs have been modified in the interests of simplicity, exactitude or clarity. In Chopin's manuscripts slurs are sometimes placed carelessly, and do not always correspond in original editions.

The editors have introduced some slight modifications of the original in the arrangement and outward appearance of the musical text. Harmonic notation and accidental signs have been altered or added where necessary, and certain changes in the distribution of notes have been effected so as to ensure the clearest visual presentation of the music, of the composer's intentions, and to safeguard the performer from hesitations, uncertainties or misunderstandings. In these cases, the editors have endeavoured to keep to the notation of the manuscripts and first editions as closely as possible, and have tried to avoid the exaggerations which sometimes characterize previous editions of Chopin's works.

For this reason also, we have very often left certain inconsistencies occurring in the notation of similar passages undisturbed. Such variants often appear in Chopin's works, not only in the notation but also in the contents of the music. Any important modification of Chopin's notation, however, has been clearly indicated in the Commentary.

In ornamentation, Chopin's original notation has been retained; attention has been drawn to any ornament appearing in different forms in the manuscripts and original editions. Wherever the execution of an ornament may give rise to doubt, the most appropriate manner has been carefully shown.

The chief difficulty lies in the method of beginning a trill. The following principles should be observed:

1) Where the principal note of a trill is preceded by an upper appoggiatura: ♪ , or by a sequence of grace notes: ♪ ♪ ♪ , the trill begins on the upper note: ♫♫♫ . In the latter case (♪), the repetition of the principal note at the beginning should be avoided.

The following: ♫♫♫ does not exist in Chopin. To obviate this mistake certain editors have added an upper appoggiatura to the notation of these trills: ♪♪

2) Where the principal note of the trill is preceded by the same note written as an appoggiatura: ![trill notation] , the trill should always begin on the principal note: ![notation] but should never be played thus: ![notation] etc.

3) Doubt may arise where the notation of the trill contains no appoggiatura. In his study *Ornamentation in the Works of F. Chopin* (London 1921, p. 1), J. P. Dunn suggests that in these cases the trill should always begin on the principal note (as if it were written: ![notation]).

Contrary to the opinion often expressed that a trill should always begin on the upper note, this principle is confirmed by the fact that Chopin sometimes writes a trill with an appoggiatura on the same pitch level as the principal note, and at other times, in a similar or corresponding place, completely omits the appoggiatura, and *vice-versa*; e. g. in the autograph of the first movement of the Sonata in B minor the trill in bar 52 is written without an appoggiatura, while the corresponding trill in the recapitulation has, in addition to the principal note, an appoggiatura on the same pitch level. There is no reason whatsoever to suppose that the second trill should be executed differently from the first.

Dunn adds (op. cit., p. 24) that the trills written without the principal note given as an appoggiatura may sometimes begin on the upper note, where this does not disturb the melodic line. Generally speaking, it can be established as a principle that in doubtful cases the trill should be started so as to link up as smoothly as possible with the preceding notes, e. g. filling a missing step or avoiding the repetition of a principal note, already performed (cf. ex. 1 and 2).

4) Difficulty may arise from the fact that Chopin sometimes used *tr* in place of the conventional sign to indicate a mordent. In the autograph MS of the Ballade in A♭ major a simple mordent sign appears in bar 3, while at the corresponding point in bar 39 Chopin has written *tr* (see also Bronisława Wójcik-Keuprulian *Melodyka Chopina*, Lwów 1930, p. 56). This is justifiable in so far as the mordent is a short form of the trill, and in a quick movement the trill is often executed as a mordent. Places where the *tr* sign may be taken to be a mordent have been indicated in the Commentary.

5) When the ending of a trill is not expressly indicated, the trill should always be completed by playing the principal note after the upper note.

6) Finally, it must be remembered that all ornaments, whether appoggiaturas, mordents, trills, turns or arpeggios, should be performed according to the accepted principle, i. e. the duration of the ornament must be subtracted from the duration of the principal note, e. g.: ![notation] is played: ![notation] or ![notation]

In Chopin's works, the signs written in his own hand in the copies of Madame Dubois, now preserved in the Library of the Paris Conservatoire (see E. Ganche *Dans le souvenir de Fr. Chopin*, Paris 1925, p. 205 et seq.), leave no doubt, from the rhythmic point of view, as to Chopin's method of executing these ornaments. There, *inter alia*, we find signs indicating that the first note of the ornament in the upper staff is to be played simultaneously with the bass note corresponding to the principal note of the ornament, e. g. in Nocturne op. 37 No. 1, and in Study op. 10 No. 3:

In this last case, the $G\sharp^1$ of the appoggiatura should be played simultaneously not only with the E in the bass, but also with the lower $G\sharp$ in the treble.

COMMENTARY

Abbreviations: FE — the original French edition (op. 29 and 51, M. Schlesinger, Paris, Nos. 2467 and 3847; op. 36, E. Troupenas, Paris, No. 892). GE — the original German edition (op. 29 and 36, Breitkopf & Härtel, Leipzig, Nos. 5850 and 6333; op. 51, F. Hofmeister, Leipzig, No. 2900). EE — the original English edition (op. 51, Wessel & Stapleton, London, No. 5304). FtE — Fontana's edition (op. 66, A. M. Schlesinger, Berlin). MS. (see below), FE, GE — original version; FE, GE and EE — original editions.

1. Impromptu in Ab major, op. 29

Chopin's autograph of this Impromptu, here designated by MS., is preserved in the Collections of the Frederick Chopin Society, Warsaw. A note written by Chopin on the title-page reads: *pour être publié le 15 octobre 1837.* (According to Niecks, a copy of FE was deposited in the Conservatoire Library in Paris in December 1837, while GE appeared in January 1838.) This autograph was used as the basis for GE, as may be inferred from the registration number 5850, which is printed on the title-page and also at the foot of each page of the latter.

The fingering marked in italics has been taken as Chopin's own from the Oxford edition; a considerable part of it is written in pencil in the copy which belonged to Madame Jędrzejewicz, Chopin's sister. In the original version, fingering is indicated only at bars 23-25; according to MS. and GE the first note of bar 23 should be played with the thumb. No fingering is shown in FE.

B a r *1.* MS. indicates *alla breve.* FE and GE have common time, ¢. In MS. and FE the first six quavers of the treble are joined in one ligature, as in the corresponding bars that occur later.

B a r *7.* Here, as at bar 89, FE has no mordent at the beginning of the bar.

B a r *11.* As the second and third quavers in the treble GE has not C^2-Db^2 but D^2-Eb^2, by analogy with the chromatic progression at bar 9. The same applies at bar 93. MS. has this version at bar 93 only.

B a r s *13–17.* The original version has one slur over these bars in the treble.

B a r *21.* In MS. and FE the quavers in the treble of this bar and bar 103 are joined by ligatures into two groups of six quavers each. There is no mordent at the beginning of these bars in FE. One has, however, been added to bar 21 in pencil in the copy that belonged to Madame Jędrzejewicz, Chopin's sister.

B a r *40.* In the original version there is no C^1 in the first bass chord.

B a r *41.* In MS. and FE the appoggiatura is given as a small crotchet.

B a r *49.* The C^1's on the first and third beats of this bar are not given in FE.

B a r *57.* The MS. notation, which we follow here, implies that the G^1 in the treble should be held throughout the bar up to the last quaver, Ab^1, to which it leads. Chopin first added two dots to the first minim (G^1), but he later suppressed them, since the same note occurs in the left hand. Nevertheless, the note should theoretically last as long as the movement of the parts would normally suggest.

B a r *64.* According to the original version, the last two crotchets in the bass are C^2-Ab^1. In the FE copy which belonged to Madame Jędrzejewicz, Chopin's sister, they have been replaced by Ab^1-F^1, as in the repetition of this passage at bar 80 of the original version.

B a r *74.* In MS. the three lower notes in the treble chord have the value of semibreves. In GE through inadvertence the stem of the upper minim, C, has been extended to include these three notes. FE has the same notation, but adds single dots to each of the four minims, while GE is in this respect an exact copy of MS. and adds a double dot only to the top note. We have adopted FE's notation, diminishing the value of the C^1, since the same note appears also in the bass, and completing the bar by the addition of a quaver rest, as has been done in more recent editions.

B a r *77.* In MS. the fourth and eleventh quavers in the treble have additional crotchet stems; in GE this is the case only with the eleventh crotchet. In FE there are no additional stems.

B a r *78.* In contrast to bar 62, MS. and GE here have the same note as an appoggiatura before the minim A^2, i. e. the trill begins on the principal note, without the initial G^2 which appears in bar 62. FE has an appoggiatura G^2 before the minim, which indicates that the trill is to be executed as at bar 62. We have adopted a uniform notation for these two bars. For the same reason we have at bar 62 added a sharp in front of the G^2 at the end of the trill (the penultimate note in the treble), to conform to bar 78 of the original version.

B a r *80.* At the beginning of this bar GE erroneously has Ab^3 instead of C^4.

B a r *121.* In FE the first chord of this bar has the value of a crotchet.

2. Impromptu in F♯ major, op. 36

MS. denotes the drafts of this Impromptu preserved in the Czartoryski Library, Cracow.

B a r *1.* GE prescribes *alla breve*, and has *Allegretto* as the tempo-marking.

B a r *14*. In FE the $B\sharp$ in the bass has only the value of a crotchet.

B a r s *31* and *35*. In GE the first quavers here and at bars 102 and 106 are prolonged by a dot instead of being followed by a semiquaver rest.

B a r s *32* and *36*. MS. and GE have $A\sharp\sharp^1$ $(A\sharp)$ instead of B^1 (B) in the bass at the beginning of these bars, as also at bar 103, though not at bar 107, where they have B. Mikuli has $A\sharp$ in all these bars, including bar 107. Since such a consistent use of the B in FE cannot be attributed to an error or to carelessness, and since the $A\sharp$ in MS. is certainly the original, the version with B should be considered as the one finally chosen by Chopin. In the chords to which we are here referring Chopin wrote E instead of $D\sharp\sharp$. We have adopted $D\sharp\sharp$, following Klindworth's edition, as this continues the progression of the parts in tenths.

B a r *37*. In contrast to MS. and GE, FE does not prolong the value of the $C\sharp$ in the bass, the third note from the end of the bar; the same applies at bar 108.

B a r *38*. In GE the first chord of this bar has the value of a minim; the same applies at bar 109. In contrast to GE, FE does not prolong the upper quaver $C\sharp$ in the bass at bar 38. In GE, in the second half of the bar, the treble is as follows:

B a r *39*. Here GE indicates *forte*. FE has no dynamic marking at all, but in the copy belonging to Madame Dubois, Chopin's pupil, *pp* is added in pencil. We have adopted this as being more appropriate, reserving *forte* for bars 47 et seq.

B a r *41*. In the penultimate chord of the right-hand part, GE lacks the dotted quaver A. In the corresponding chord at bar 49 GE has an A^1, which is, however, tied to the preceding semiquaver A^1. This tie does not appear in FE.

B a r *50*. In GE the bass of the second half of the bar is notated as follows:

The same version is given in Mikuli's edition.

B a r *53*. According to FE the treble of the second half of the bar is as follows:

This version creates a clash with the bass; for this reason we have chosen GE's version.

B a r s *53—57*. GE has no semiquaver rests in the bass, which maintains the notation of bars 51—52.

B a r *58*. GE has no B^1 in the first chord of the bar.

B a r *72*. In GE the last note in the treble is shortened to a semiquaver following a dotted quaver.

B a r *74*. In GE, the first three notes of the treble $(E\sharp\sharp^2\text{-}D\sharp\sharp^2\text{-}B^1)$ are written as a triplet of three equal quavers, while in FE the $E\sharp\sharp^2$ is written as an appoggiatura. Mikuli has a long appoggiatura.

B a r s *75* and *76*. In GE a crotchet stem has been added to the first and seventh quavers in the treble of bar 75; at bar 76 the seventh note in the treble is written simultaneously as a quaver and as a minim.

B a r s *78, 79* and *81*. In GE a crotchet stem is added to the first and fourth quavers in the treble.

B a r *80*. GE has $A\sharp\sharp^1\text{-}D\sharp\sharp^2\text{-}F\sharp\sharp^2$ as the second triplet in the treble instead of the $A\sharp\sharp^1\text{-}B^1\text{-}D\sharp\sharp^2$ given in FE and Mikuli.

B a r *84*. In GE the last note in the bass is a semiquaver following a dotted quaver. In the corresponding passage at bar 90 GE has two equal quavers, but at bar 91, as at bar 84, the last $G\sharp$ in the bass is written as a semiquaver after a dotted A. FE has equal quavers throughout all the corresponding passages, while Mikuli gives the dotted rhythm.

B a r *87*. As the fourth quaver in the bass GE has the chord $F\sharp\text{-}G\sharp\text{-}D\sharp^1$.

B a r *89*. In GE and Mikuli's edition the last five notes in the treble are the same as at bar 83. FE has the following variant:

B a r s *92—93*. In FE the last notes in the treble in bar 92 and the first in bar 93 are as follows:

B a r s *94* and *96*. The slur over the two $G\sharp$'s (the second and third quavers in the bass) probably means not that the first of them should be held, but that the two notes should be played *legato*, like those that follow an octave higher in the same bar.

B a r *95*. In GE the $F\sharp$ in the bass is given not as a syncopated note coming on the second quaver of the bar but as the third quaver, following a quaver rest. In GE and in Mikuli's edition the nineteenth note in the treble is an E^1, as at bar 97, where MS. also has an E^1. In both cases FE has a sharp: this was probably added later, witness the fact that there is a sharp before the third last note in the treble, which with the addition of the others become redundant but which remained, presumably inadvertently, unchanged. In Mikuli's edition the first four notes in the treble at bar 95 are the same as at bar 97.

B a r *96*. GE has the fifth *D♯* in addition to the octave *C♯-C♯* on the second quaver in the bass, as at bar 94; on the sixth quaver in the bass it also has the fifth *D♯¹*.

B a r *97*. In GE the first four notes in the treble are the same as at bar 95, but the tenth *A♯²* has been added to the fifth *F♯¹-C♯²* in the left-hand part at the beginning of the bar. In MS. and in GE the penultimate group of four demisemiquavers (in the treble) consists of the notes *C♯¹-F♯¹-G♯¹-A♯¹*. FE has no lower *C♯* (the last quaver in the bass).

B a r *101*. In MS. and FE the first note in the treble has the value of a crotchet.

3. *Impromptu in G♭ major, op. 51*

B a r *1*. In GE *tempo giusto* is prescribed, and the title is given as *Allegro vivace. Impromptu*, but on the cover there is only *Allegro vivace pour le pianoforte*, without the word *Impromptu*. FE has *Troisième Impromptu* as the title and, like EE, gives the tempo as *Vivace*. The piece should not be played too quickly.

B a r *6*. In FE and EE the third quaver in the treble is *C♭²* and not *A♭¹*. In the corresponding passage in the recapitulation (bar 79), both editions have *A♭¹*.

B a r *13*. FE and EE lack the appoggiatura *G♭¹* before the sixth quaver in the treble; it appears only at bars 29 and 86.

B a r *14*. GE has a mordent on the second note of the treble, as also at bars 30 and 87. These mordents are not given in FE and EE. We have adopted GE's version.

B a r s *20—22*. In FE and GE the appoggiaturas in the treble are written as small quavers.

B a r s *23—24*. In the original editions the slurs in these bars end on the last quaver in the treble.

B a r *25*. In the original editions the last chord in the bass has no naturals. Recent editions, among them Mikuli's, add naturals, by analogy with bar 9. As for the distribution of the notes, we have followed the original editions, but recommend that the lower note in the right-hand (*B♭¹*) should be joined to the last chord in the left hand, as at bar 9.

B a r *32*. In the copy belonging to Madame Dubois, Chopin's pupil, the slurs here and at bars 33, 34 and 37 have been altered in pencil: they end on the last note of each bar. The same applies in the recapitulation.

B a r *33*. The original editions have a *crescendo* sign here instead of *diminuendo*. As these editions prescribe *diminuendo* in all subsequent corresponding bars, we have given the same sign here.

B a r s *37* and *38*. The use of the thumb six times in succession in the treble was prescribed by Chopin himself. From this fingering it follows that *G♭¹* and *A♭¹* should be held with the second and third fingers. Mikuli shifts the pause from the end of bar 38 to the penultimate note in the treble (*A♭¹*).

B a r s *42* and *44*. At bar 42 in the original editions the slur begins on the second note of the treble. The initial *A♭¹* must therefore be considered as closing the phrase begun in the previous bar. We have adopted this phrasing for bar 44 as well, although the original editions begin the slur in the treble on the first note of this bar. These remarks apply also to bars 99 and 101.

B a r *49*. *Alla breve* is prescribed here by Mikuli and the critical edition of Breitkopf & Härtel. We have adopted the time signature given in the original editions.

B a r s *53* and *54*. The following notation seems more appropriate for the treble in these bars:

Similarly, the following notes should also be written as crotchets: *B♭¹* and *F¹* in bar 55, *A♭¹* in bar 62, *F¹* and *C¹* in bar 63, etc.

B a r *59*. In GE crotchet stems are added to the first notes of the first three quaver groups in the treble, as in the fourth group.

B a r *82*. As at bar 25, we have here followed the version given in the original editions, in particular that of FE. In GE and EE the upper *A♭¹* in the penultimate chord does not share a stem with the lower notes, *A♭-D♭¹*. As for the execution of this bar, we recommend that the version given for bar 9 should be kept here.

4. *Fantaisie - Impromptu in C♯ minor op. posth. (66)*

The approximate date of the composition of this work (1834) is given by Fontana. Probably it was also he who added the term *Fantaisie* to the title.

B a r *12*. The following slurring would be more appropriate:

B a r s *13—24*. In bars 13—16 FtE has short slurs over the successive groups of four semiquavers. We have added longer slurs to indicate the phrasing. FtE has no slurs in bars 17—24. In bars 13—16, Klindworth adds a crotchet stem to the accented first semiquavers of each four-note group in the treble, and in bars 17—20 to the accented second semiquavers of the corresponding groups. This is, in fact, the way most pianists execute this passage in a quick tempo. In bars 21—22 Klindworth emphasizes all the first and second semiquavers in the four-note groups in a similar way, while in bars 23—24 he emphasizes only the first semiquavers.

B a r s *16* and *22*. FtE has no accents here or in the recapitulation (bars 94 and 100).

B a r *41*. In FtE there is no signature to indicate the change of time. Similarly the return to *alla breve* at bar 83 is omitted.

B a r s *41* and *42*. In FtE the highest note in these bars, F^1, is written on the upper staff, probably in order to indicate that it should be played with the right hand.

B a r *43*. Certain more recent editions give the metronome marking as $\downarrow$ = 88. Here and at bars 47, 51, 55 etc. the *tr.* sign indicates a mordent, as it so frequently does in Chopin.

B a r s *43—82*. In this section we have completed or changed the slurs in the treble; in FtE they are often incorrect and inconsistent.

B a r *44*. According to FtE it is not only the $A\flat^1$ in the bass figuration that appears in the upper staff, but also both the neighbouring F^1's. According to Mikuli this $A\flat^1$ should be played with the right hand.

B a r s *49; 57* and similar bars. Considered in relation to the general pattern of the melodic line, the turns in these bars scarcely seem to be in Chopin's style; the question therefore arises as to whether Chopin did not mark them with the usual signs which afterwards, when transcribed in full by Fontana, were misinterpreted, especially since it is quite probable that Chopin himself *made a mistake and used an incorrect sign* to denote a turn (cf. B. Wójcik-Keuprulian *Melodyka Chopina*, Lwów 1930, p. 70 et seq.; this author also remarks that the turn beginning on the upper note is much more frequent in Chopin than the other kind, v. ibid. p. 67). The following turns would seem to us to be much more in Chopin's style:

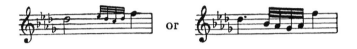

But, of course, only the manuscripts could solve this problem.

B a r *53*. In this bar, as in later corresponding bars, Klidworth adds crotchet stems to the accented quavers in the bass; this is further justified by the fact that the third quaver from the end in the preceding bar has a crotchet stem which is added in FtE.

B a r s *65* and *77*. In contrast to bar 53, the turn here is notated in demisemiquavers.

B a r s *119—124*. In FtE there are no long slurs in the treble. Klindworth adds crotchet stems to the accented semiquavers in these bars, as in bars 13 et seq. At bars 119, 121 and 123, FtE has *ff* at the beginning of each bar. We have withheld the sign *f* until the second group of semiquavers.

DR LUDWIK BRONARSKI
Fribourg (Switzerland)
PROF. JÓZEF TURCZYŃSKI
Morges